This Guita[r Can Talk]
By Tom Long
(with Mike Stewart)

THIS GUITAR CAN TALK

Chapter 1. Vietnam

On February 28, 1968 I returned from a one year tour in Viet Nam. During that year I had a three piece band which got me out of the jungle on weekends to play Enlisted Men Clubs and Officers Clubs throughout Viet Nam. Since I was in a

Figure 1- Kula Gulf Aircraft Carrier

Huey Helicopter outfit, I was able to make friends with high ranking officers who really liked our music and agreed to fly Larry Peters, Johnny Carlisle and I to various parts of the country to perform.

Prior to leaving San Francisco on old World War II aircraft carrier "The Kula Gulf", I purchased an old Harmony F Hole Guitar to help keep me company for the long ship ride. My MOS was "helicopter electrician, and I was to escort 33 Boeing Vertol Chinooks all the way to Vung Tau Harbor. For over a week we put blades back on the big choppers and then flew them off the deck to a place in the jungle called Bearcat. Here we pitched tents, built bunkers and outhouses and make shift showers. During our down time I was always playing this old 2nd hand guitar and drawing attention from surrounding tents which developed into small concerts.

Figure 2 - Sgt. Boone, Tom Long, Larry Peters, Vietnam

After a few weeks of in company performing, Sgt. Boone from the 200th Assault Helicopter company offered to get his commanding officer to fly us to Vung Tau to play, then Soc Trane and other places up north near the DMZ. We were offered a gig to play with Bob Hope while he was in country in May of 1967, but it never worked out due to us not having the proper equipment. Prior to leaving Vietnam on Feb. 28th 1968 I sold my old Harmony to another GI and regret that decision to this day.

After returning state side and being discharged on June 21st 1968 at Hunter

Airfield in Savannah, Ga., I married my high school girl friend, had two children and after 5 years was divorced and searching what life had in store for me. I had returned to my old job at Lockheed Aircraft but was laid off in 1972 and I wasn't sure what to do next. My only salvation at that time was music and this lead me one day to Ken Stanton Music in Marietta, Ga. where I bought a FG 180 Yamaha Guitar from an old friend, Ken Biddy, who worked there. I cherished this guitar and the sweet deep sound that it made.

Right after being laid off from Lockheed and going through my divorce, I went to Daytona Beach Fla. with my friend, Danny Wilbur, who unknown to us, was dying due to cancer developed from Agent Orange. Danny was in the Marines in Vietnam and was exposed a great deal to the chemical while he was there. This trip in 1973 really changed my life. I saw that Johnny Carver was appearing at the Torch Light Lounge. He had a hit at the time called "Tie A Yellow Ribbon Around The Old Oak Tree". Danny & I went to the show that night and I saw the most beautiful girl that I had ever seen, Belinda Gail Tanner, from Mobile, Alabama. I honestly believe that God had his hand on that night. Belinda and I started dating long distance from Marietta, Ga. to Mobile over several months and then she got a job in Atlanta and moved to be closer to me. We married Feb. 28th 1976 in Smyrna, Ga. in a small wedding chapel and the cost was only $100.00. This included a small reception and giving the preacher $25.00. We had no money, but I felt so alive with a woman I loved and a new guitar that seemed to be my 2nd best friend.

What made this relationship more meaningful was that right after Belinda moved to Georgia, I got into some trouble with a couple of guys who were a bad influence on me and caused me to spend a little time in the county jail. Upon my release, it was hard getting a job, although I had a college degree in business management from Ga. State University and Belinda stood by me thru it all . This led to a job at Perfection Sound Studios in Smyrna, Ga, right down the street from where our apartment was located. This job inspired me to go back to college at

Ga. State and get a degree in commercial music which led to an internship job at Master Sound Studios and then onto the Lowery Music Group.

While at Master Sound, which was located on Spring Street in Atlanta, I began to meet many famous people who were there recording or doing voice commercials for major companies. One such person was Ted Williams, the famous baseball player, who was doing a series of Sears commercials. He actually knocked me down one day with the door coming out to studio B . He reached down to pick me up and all I could say was ....you're Ted Williams!....Later I thought, why didn't I get his autograph or signature on my guitar. Anyway, this is where my FG180 Guitar starts it's journey of acquiring all the 200 plus signatures that it holds today which are scratched into the wood grain.

CHAPTER 2
ISSAC HAYES

One day I came into the studio at Master Sound and Issac Hayes was writing songs on the grand piano for his new album. After several days around Issac, I got the bright idea to have him sign my FG180 guitar...The only pen around was a regular fountain pen so that's what he used and scratched his name into the grain which lead me to have everyone else from that point on to do the same. After this, Issac invited Belinda and I to his house for dinner and man what a house! It was located across the street from the Governor's mansion on West Paces Ferry Rd. Issac had just moved into the new house and it was almost empty except for a dining room table. I never will forget how impressed Belinda was with the huge chandelier in the bathroom.

Figure 3 - Issac Hayes, Belinda and Tom Long

After a couple of years at Master Sound, I went to work for Bill Lowery as a song plugger. Working for Bill, enabled me to get more signatures on my FG180 because he had discovered many famous writers and artists. Along about this time I co-founded the Atlanta Songwriters Association with my good friends Larry Latimer ,who wrote the "Nothing Runs Like A Deer" jingle which became so famous for the John Deere company and Steven Weaver who became a very in demand entertainment attorney and was the director then of the Commercial Music Dept. at Georgia State University.

Issac Hayes was very kind to me ,but running into Mr. Hayes at Master Sound was not my first encounter with him...After spending my time with the Cobb County authority , I landed a job at the Atlanta International Hotel owned by Senator Leroy Johnson who was a wealthy black man...Since I had a management degree, he made me the Credit manager of the hotel....

My first challenge at that time was to collect money owed the hotel by guest who the Senator hated to just kick out...The first guest who owed $14,000 in room charges was...you guessed it....Issac Hayes....I was able
to get $7,000 from him with the promise to pay the rest when his album was finished.....After this encounter with trying to collect money, I saw that this job was not for me, and quit the next week....Was I surprised to see him again when I started my intern at Master Sound....

Chapter 3
Joe South

Joe South signed my guitar while I worked at the Lowery Group along with many of his friends like Tommy Roe, Ray Whitley and Freddy Weller.

Figure 4 - Joe South, Belinda and Tom

I focus this chapter mainly on Joe because he was Bill Lowery's most productive writer over the years Bill was in business. Joe was one of my all time writer hero's. He wrote "I Never Promised You A Rose Garden", "Games People Play", "Walk A Mile In My Shoes", "Down In The Boondocks", "Hush" and so many more all by himself. This lead to a great friendship which lasted until his death in Sept. 2012. After the Georgia Music Hall of Fame closed down in June of 2011, I was able to help Joe Chambers, the owner of the Musician's Hall Of Fame in Nashville, to acquire two of Joe's guitars that he wrote all of his hits on.

Joe has those displayed in the new Musician's Hall of Fame located in the old Municipal Auditorium which takes up 60,000 sq. feet. In addition to this, the Musician's Hall also has on display Bill Lowery's office just as it was all the years he published all those great songs...

Chapter 4
Tree Days

In December of 1980, Buddy Killen who owned Tree publishing hired me away from Bill Lowery and Belinda and I moved to Nashville to be a song plugger for the biggest country music publishing company in the world. When I went for my interview with Buddy prior to moving he asked me how much money I would need per week...I only made $150.00 per week with Bill so I ask for twice that much....He told me he would have paid me $500 per week if I had ask...This position put me

Figure 5 - Tom, Buddy Killen, Dan Wilson

around many of my country hero's that I
admired so much, like Harlan Howard,
Hank Cochran, Curly Putman, Red Lane,
Sonny Throckmorton and Roger Miller.
There are so many stories it's hard to
remember them all, but the next three
years at Tree was probably the best years
of my musical career. It's unfortunate
that I didn't get pictures of many of these
hero's signing my guitar, but I'm glad I
was able to get a few of the great ones.

Harlan Howard was famous for his three
chords and the truth philosophy. At one

time during his career he had over 10 songs in the top 20 in one given week. He wrote and co-wrote hits such as "Tiger By The Tail" for Buck Owens, "Busted" for Ray Charles, "Heartache By The Number" and 100's of other great songs. I was fortunate to help Harlan produce some of his demo's, but one great story when he signed my guitar was the day Conway Twitty was in the Tree building. Conway came in that day in his old jogging outfit to play us all his Twitty Bird project which was directed at the children's market. It was sort like the chip monks but was a little bird singing and talking.

Figure 6 - Tom's office at Tree Publishing

After we sat for over 45 minutes listening to this little bird, Harlan walks in the room and tells Conway he has a new song for him to hear. We put the cassette in the player and listen to "He Don't Know a Thing About Love". He, meaning the Moon in this title. Harlan and been fishing on Center Hill Lake one night when the moon was full and the fish were not biting. Therefore the idea hit him to write a song about the moon that was shining down so bright on his fishing habit. Conway took a copy of the song that day and it went on to be a #1 country song for Conway. This was the day that Harlan signed my guitar and I will never forget the line in that song that says....He don't know a thing about love, He just hangs up above....

Chapter 5
Red Lane

Red was Merle Haggard's guitar player for several years and became a good friend when I came to Tree. He had many hits as well but one that I really loved was "Miss Emily's Picture" that John Conlee had a hit with.

I was sitting in my office one day which was right next to Red's office. He had his door closed writing, and my phone rings....Hey, it's Red,...Come over here and tell me what you think about this new song.. I stepped into his office and there sat Red with his feet up on his desk, his chair leaned back with his gut string guitar up on his chest. He starts playing his new creation and I just sat there with my mouth open...All I could say was....WOW.. A classic ......John Conlee took it all the way to #1. Red signed my guitar that day...what a memory....

Chapter 6
Roger Miller

Roger was in Curly Putnam's office one afternoon right after a celebration for his broadway musical "Big River". I was hanging out with them talking about their younger days and how they met and the memories of drinking at Tootsies Orchard Lounge. This was the day that Roger signed my guitar in big bold block letters. I think he was on some medication at the time for his throat cancer, which he died from a few years later, or it could have been something else, however he was so funny and had the quickest wit I had ever been around. I was with Roger one other time at Larry Butler's ranch out on Nolensville Rd. for Buddy Killen's 50th birthday party right after I moved to Nashville. We were sitting in Larry's kitchen admiring his collection of colt 45 pistols which were in glass cases and I was just on cloud nine being in the same room with him and Larry...Larry was the first producer to ever win a Grammy from Nashville for producing the Gambler album on Kenny Rogers...Roger also signed my "Big River" album which like a fool I sold on Ebay back in 2012....Roger

Miller, was no doubt king of the road and king of wit in the country music world.....One of a kind and who else could ever write a song like "Can't Roller Skate In A Buffalo Herd" and get it played on country radio....

Figure 7 - Curly Putnam and Roger Miller

Chapter 7
Curly Putman

Mr. "Green Green Grass Of Home" who was the go to writer at Tree if you could not finish a song or get it just right...Curly and I became fast friends and I'm sure lots of writers in Nashville would say the same thing. He was always so kind and would always take me to lunch and spend quality time with me. I regret never writing a song with him, but I was always so comfortable just being his friend and enjoying our fellowship and stories.

Figure 8 – Harlan Howard and Curly Putnam

Curly co-wrote "He Stop Loving Her Today" with Bobby Braddock which was voted the best country song ever written. His song " Green Green Grass Of Home" has been recorded well over 600 times and earned Curly well over 6 million dollars. Other songs he wrote are "My Elusive Dreams", "D-I-V-O-R-C-E, " I Wish I Could Hurt That Way Again", "It's A Cheating Situation" and many more....

Belinda & I became close friends with Curly and his wife Bernice, going to their house for dinner and sitting with them during Tree Christmas parties at The Hillwood Country Club. One year when Paul McCartney and Wings came to Nashville they rented Curly's big farm house in Lebanon ,Tennessee as a place to stay while they recorded an album on Music Row. Paul sent Curly & family to Hawaii for over a month all expenses paid while they took over the Putman Estate with their young kids. After returning from Hawaii, Curly found out that Paul's kids had wrote on the walls of their house and messed up the carpets. Paul had the house totally redecorated with new paint and new carpet. Needless to say, Curly and Paul became good friends and people are still talking about the month Paul McCartney stayed in Lebanon, Tennessee. Curly signed my guitar that same day that Roger Miller did in Curly's office...Curly still lives in Lebanon, Tn. in the same house and we still stay in touch by phone and go to lunch when I'm back in Nashville....

Chapter 8
Sonny Throckmorton

Puddin' as we all called him, was the most interesting and unique writer I encountered during my 3 years at Tree Publishing. I had met Sonny prior to moving to Nashville when I worked for The Lowery Music Group. Bill Lowery use to send me to Nashville once a month to pitch his catalog of songs. I would stay at the Best Western Hall of Fame Motor Inn on Division Street which was right across the street from

Figure 9 - Sonny Throckmorton

Harold Shedd's original Music Mill Studio. Before I started my trips to Nashville, Mr. Lowery, who was the President of the Atlanta Chapter of NARAS (National Academy of Recording Arts & Science) and The Country Music Association ,sent letters to all the important people on music row introducing me as his new song plugger or creative manager.
He also told me to take a stack of Joe South songbooks and hand out to people as they let me in their door. Sometimes I

would just knock on the door, introduce myself as working for Bill Lowery and present them with a songbook. During those rounds I always stopped by Tree Publishing and after a few visits they let me hang out on the 2nd floor where all the writer rooms were and all the songwriter offices were located. On one lucky day I ran into Sonny and he was real friendly to me since I knew several of his hits like..."Friday Night Blues", "The Way I Am", "I Wish I Was Eighteen Again", "Knee Deep In Love" and "It's A Cheating Situation". Sonny signed my guitar that day and he was the first one to sign it on the back of the guitar. He made his signature so big it took up most of the back middle part of the guitar. He does have a long last name, so I think he was just needing more room and the back was blank at that time.

Sonny loved to smoke grass and he always kept two different kinds in his office stashed up in the ceiling on top of those removable ceiling tiles. He had one kind for writing, which was laced with something, and another kind for just partying. He had the most unique laugh I had ever heard. Sounded sort of like a goose calling it's mate...Later on Sonny bought my pickup truck that I used to move to Nashville in along with a camper shell that was removable. After he bought the truck, he and Bruce Channel ("Hey Baby" fame) rode down to my house in Smyrna, Tn. to put the shell back on the truck. Well, when we got there, which was a hot July day, Sonny sat in my carport smoking a joint while Bruce and I put the camper shell back on the truck. All Sonny could do was sit there in the shade and give us his big Ole funny laugh while Bruce and I were sweating trying to fit all the screws and clamps on to secure the camper top. I really don't know how Sonny was able to drive that truck back to his farm in Lebanon ,Tn. where he lived in his condition. I guess he was immune...

Chapter 9
Hank Cochran

My first office at Tree Publishing was in the 2nd floor board room until a real office became available...After a few weeks Hank Cochran decided he didn't need an office anymore and ask me if I would like to have his space. I said sure, and noticed this big framed poster style picture of Willie Nelson hanging on his wall with Willie standing in a wheat field with a wheat straw in his mouth. I said, Hank, that a cool picture of Willie...He said yea, it's one of Willie promoting his line of Willie Jeans. Then I noticed his name Willie on the back pocket. I started to help Hank take some things from his office when he said....leave Willie's picture on the wall...It's yours....just get me a cut...

Hank was called the Legend by many and he and Willie Nelson were close friends...When Hank worked for Pamper Music he signed Willie as a writer when Willie first came to Nashville....Later, Tree bought the Pamper catalog and that's how they acquired Willie as a writer and many

Figure 10 - Hank Cochran Songbook

of his early songs.. Hank had a big boat
down in the Caribbean Islands and he
named the boat The Legend....He often
would take Red Lane, Willie and many of
his artist buddies down to fish, write and
just hang out. He got lots of cuts that way
with the artists he entertained. A few
years after I left Tree, Willie was in
Nashville recording a new project and I
got my friend, Herky Williams, who
worked with Willie some, to take that

picture to the studio and Willie signed it for me. Hank signed my guitar the day he gave me the Willie picture...I was thrilled twice in one day....

Some of Hank's big songs are: "Make The World Go Away" sung by Eddie Arnold and many other artitsts, "I Fall To Pieces" by Pasty Cline, "A Little Biddy Tear Let Me Down" by Burl Ives, and so many more. Hank was an avid reader and a good friend who died of cancer back in 2011.....

Chapter 10
Buck Owens

Buck Owens was one of my early hero's and I just loved his sound that was so different than the other Nashville artists. I use to go buy his 45 records when they came out back in the 60's like "Santa Looked A Lot Like Daddy" , "Together Again", and "I've Got A Tiger By The Tail" which he co-wrote with Harlan Howard.

I first saw Buck & the Buckaroos in Marietta, Ga. when they sang at a "K-Mart store opening on Roswell Rd. near the Big Chicken right off highway 41. I will never forget that day. The Beatles were red hot then and K-Mart had a flat bed trailer set up right in front of the main doors. A huge crowd had gathered and when the doors opened, the Buckaroos came out dressed like the Beatles, hair and all. They kicked off the show with "I want to hold your hand" and the crowd went wild. Then they pulled off their mop hair wigs and struck up with "I've Got A Tiger By The Tail". I was so amazed at their tight sound and all those awesome licks Don Rich did on his telecaster guitar.

Fast forward twenty years later and I'm sitting in my office at Tree Publishing. Buck Owens comes into my office with Harlan Howard and we had a great talk about his Blue Book catalog that Tree Publishing was buying that day for 2 million dollars. I told Buck about that day at the K-Mart store and how everyone was so surprised with the Beatles opening. We had a big laugh and he really impressed me with his knowledge of radio and informed me that he owned several radio stations. What a great deal Buddy Killen made that day when Buck signed the paperwork giving Tree ownership of that great catalog and what a happy day it was for me because Buck also signed my guitar with the same pen he just made 2 million dollar with..

Chapter 11
Dean Dillon

The writer that has more songs recorded by George Strait than any other writer. I think to date Dean has had over 40 songs recorded by George and has had over 30 plus singles. George has made Dean millions of dollars and he has spent a great deal of that amount on different wives and drugs over the earlier years of his life.

Figure 11 - Dean Dillion

Figure 12 - Tom and Dean

Thank God he has gotten his life somewhat in order over the past 10 years. I was fortunate to write a few songs with Dean in the early 80's and he recorded one that we co-wrote with the late Frank Knapp on his Brotherly Love album on RCA Records as a duet with Gary Stewart. It's called "Suburban Life" and that album now is kind of a classic especially in Europe. A few of my favorite Dean Dillon song are: "The Chair", "UnWound", "Nobody In His Right Mind Would Have Left Her", and "Marina Del-Ray". Dean is a western looking type character sort of like Buffalo Bill Cody.

One of my fondest memories of Dean was at a demo session I was producing at Tree one morning back in 1982. The players were booked and in the studio for a 10 a.m. start time. It was Dean's session and he was nowhere to be found. The clock was ticking and it's 10:30, then 10:45 and I'm about to tell the players that the sessions was cancelled because Dean was a no show...About that time the back door near the studio comes flying open and in comes a luggage rack from the Spence Manor Hotel next door with Gary Stewart on the bottom, Tanya Tucker laying across the top and Dean pushing. They had been partying all night at the Spence Manor with Glen Campbell and Glen had knocked Tanya's two front caps completely out of her mouth. She was stoned and locked herself in my office and wouldn't come out. After about 30 minutes Dean convinced her to open the door and the musicians stayed and we actually finished the demo session on time and finished at 1pm. Since I had all three of their attentions that morning, Dean, Gary and

Tanya signed my guitar ..What a morning in one day of country music..

Chapter 12
Dolly Parton

The very first picture I ever got of someone signing my Guitar was Dolly on the 2nd floor of Tree Publishing Company. I had always been a huge fan and appreciated the fact that she came from a poor family in the eastern part of Tennessee next to the smoky mountains. Her family had great hard working values and I respected that very much. Dolly knew what she wanted early in life and she was bound and determined to make her dream come true.

Figure 13 - Dolly Parton and Tom

She had a God given talent to write songs, she was pretty, and she could really belt out a tune from that tiny frame.

The day Dolly signed my FG-180 guitar she was at Tree to do an administration deal with Buddy Killen of all her great songs. Buddy was the first person to sign Dolly to a publishing deal and she respected his ability to get songs cut and collect royalties. We made many group pictures that day, but I was able to corner her in Sonny Throckmorton's office and she gladly signed and agreed to a picture which I cherish very much....Dolly was a little heavier back then and later I found out that we are the same age. What a country music Icon she is and two of my favorite songs she wrote are: "I Will Always Love You", and "The Coat Of Many Colors".

Chapter 13
Emmylou Harris

I'm not real sure why Emmylou came to Tree on the day she signed my guitar. It was so long ago, but I think she was there to celebrate a song she had recorded by one of the tree writers and we all had on I Love You Emmylou T shirts.

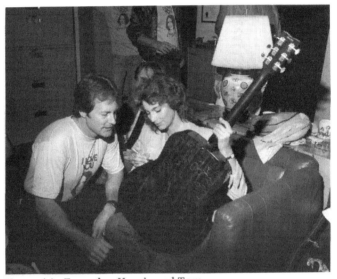

Figure 14 - Emmylou Harris and Tom

She was a huge star at the time with hits in various markets and I was thrilled to have her sign my FG-180 and get a picture of the occasion. I guess my favorite recording by her was "Two More Bottles

Of Wine"...She was almost instrumental in the careers of Vince Gill and producer Tony Brown who has produced just about everyone in Nashville. When Tony got his job at RCA Records in the A&R dept. Jerry Bradley, who was the V.P. under Chet Atkins, played a real funny trick on Tony. You see, Tony is very short in stature and Jerry had all this small furniture put in Tony's new office and put the door knob real low on the door. When Tony arrived for his first day, he was pretty shocked and everyone in the office got a great laugh....They only did it, because they knew he would be very successful at his new position and he was good at taking jokes.

Chapter 14
Transition period

Those Tree Publishing days only lasted 3 years before I would leave and go to work for the American Society of Composers, Authors, and Publishers, better know as ASCAP. I think this came about because in 1983 I was elected President of the Nashville Songwriters Association International, better known as NSAI who today owns the Blue Bird Café which is so famous.. During that year I was at a lot of functions,, spoke at Award Dinners and was on National T.V., (The Music City News Awards) presenting Ray Stevens with an award. This was a great year for me, because it threw me center stage with the top writers & artists in country music. During the Nashville Songwriters Hall of Fame dinners, all the performing rights organizations were present. This included Francis Preston from BMI, Hal David from ASCAP, the oldest PRO formed in 1914, and Diane Petty from SESAC. I was the host for these events and always introduced by the executive director, Mrs. Maggie Cavender, who was one of the cofounders of the NSAI. Maggie liked me very much and was very instrumental in be being elected as President of the organization. I would often travel to New York, Dallas Texas, Los Angeles and Atlanta with Maggie to be on panels or at other songwriter events. I mentioned all the above because it leads me the point of a major career change for me. Hal David, President of ASCAP, who was a very successful Pop songwriter with songs such as "Raindrops Keep Falling On My Head" and many of Dion Warwick's hits, approached me one day and ask if I would consider working for ASCAP. He told me that Connie Bradley, the head of the Nashville office was thinking about leaving in a couple of years and wanted to groom me for her position. After much soul searching and counsel from Roger Sovine, I accepted the position which lasted for 10 years. During this time I was able to get many of the young up and coming writers and artists to sign my guitar and thanks to Alan Mayor, some great pictures of the signings...

Chapter 15
Alan Jackson

Being from Georgia I was excited when a new comer from Newnan, Georgia was climbing the charts and decided to join ASCAP. Alan had signed with the newly formed Arista Records country division headed up by my friend Tim DuBois who had produced and managed a band called Restless Heart. Tim was from Oklahoma and had an accounting degree but loved to write songs and was once a staff writer at Bob Montgomery's House of Gold co-owned by Bobby Goldsboro and Kenny O'Dell. Tim put together quite an operation at Arista and Alan would become the superstar he is today with the help of that well oiled machine.

Figure 15 - Alan Jackson and Tom

Early in his career, ASCAP was still doing luncheons for the country radio seminar event at the Opryland Hotel, and we would usually present an artist writer that was becoming popular. I'm not sure of the year, but we had Alan Jackson on the luncheon show and all the DJ's loved Alan and I think that day really helped him seal the deal with the radio industry. When Alan had his first #1 party at ASCAP I was able to get him to sign my guitar and Alan Mayor shot a picture of us together with my guitar. We had several #1 parties for Alan while I was at ASCAP over my 10 year tenure, but on one occasion I will never forget. Alan didn't have much hair early on in his career, and after the new ASCAP building was completed we had a party for him and the building was packed with music row folks. Finally when Alan and Denise, his wife, walked in the back door, Alan sort of bows, takes off his cowboy hat and shows off his new transplanted blond locks. Everyone cheered and clapped. I guess some folks didn't realize that all this time early on he was thin on the head....

Chapter 16
Garth Brooks

I had the opportunity to be around Garth numerous times early on before he had a record deal.

Figure 16 Tom and Garth Brooks

Bob Doyle, who became Garth's manager and publisher actually discovered Garth, while he and I worked at ASCAP together. Garth was from Oklahoma and had come to Nashville prior to moving to music city. He once met with Merlin Littlefield at

ASCAP who told Garth his songs were not yet ready and good enough to compete and that he should go back to Oklahoma and develop some more. I think Garth took this to heart and it gave him the burning desire to become better and he returned in the late 80's with Sandi his wife to make his mark that would not be erased. He and Sandi both worked at a boot store near Hendersonville making rent money while Garth started to make his rounds and co-write with anyone that would listen to what hooks he had under his cowboy hat. I remember him coming into the ASCAP office meeting with Bob Doyle on numerous occasions. Bob would often play me some of his songs and I really didn't hear anything at that time I felt was different and unique. My thoughts changed however, one night at the Sutler Cafe on 8th avenue. Belinda and I went with Bob to hear Garth and I bet there were only about 10 people in the whole place. That night made me a believer. He got up on that little stage with his cowboy hat and guitar and after a couple songs I saw what Bob had been telling everyone. The passion in his eyes and voice told me this cowboy was definitely different and he had what people call the X factor.

During this time I had a new 1986 Astro Van and Belinda and I took Garth and Sandi to dinner one night at the Go-10 Japanese restaurant in Nashville. We had a great time just getting to know each other better. Bob Doyle and his girl friend Pat Wood joined us there. Garth had been turned down by every label in town a couple of times but one magic night at the Bluebird Café Garth sat in for Ralph Murphy who had to cancel, and Lynn Shultz from Capitol Records was in the audience and he knew his boss Jim Foglesong had to sign him. Mr. Foglesong did and the rest you could say is history. He went on to be the biggest selling country artist ever. Boy Doyle still manages Garth to this day and is still his publisher.

Another story about Garth and Bob before I get to him signing my guitar. Bob Doyle was a major in the Tennessee Air National Guard and he flew C-130 airplanes on the weekends to make extra money which he needed after his divorce. I think he earned about $200 each time he flew.

Bob was a jet pilot in the Air Force and continued with the Guard when he got out of full time service. Anyway, Bob signed Garth to a publishing deal kind of under the table while working at ASCAP and was paying Garth $100.00 per week to write. In order to pay this, Bob started flying extra sorties each week to cover the draw he was giving Garth. After about one year of this, Bob decided to take the plunge and go full time as Garth's publisher. He set up Major Bob Music (ASCAP) and I helped him move into his little rented office down the street next to Chet Atkins building which was on 17th avenue or Music Square West which it's referred to now. Connie Bradley, the head of ASCAP in Nashville, gave Bob a typewriter and some old furniture we didn't need at the ASCAP office and he was off on a wing and a prayer. Bob tried his best at the time to get Nashville writers to co-write with Garth, but most of the well known tunesmiths at the time didn't want to waste their time on a new up and comer. The ones that did invest their time however, like Kent Blazy, Kim Williams, and Pat Alger later became millionaires from the songs they penned together.

Bob Doyle also tried his best to get Garth a manager and a record producer, but could not get any interest at first. Bob was very frustrated and decided to just manager Garth on his own and finally got his friend Allen Reynolds interested enough to take a stab at producing Garth. Garth is a very loyal person and through all the years of people like Jimmy Bowen trying to sway Garth to let him produce and get other high profile managers to take over his career, Garth has stuck with who brought him to the dance. Needless to say just about everyone in the so called Garth inner circle have become wealthy people and most of those folks from his business agent Kerry O'Neil to his lawyer, Rusty Jones, are still in the mix.

ASCAP had many #1 parties for Garth and you never knew how he would look when he showed up at the over crowed functions. One event in the new ASCAP building at 2 Music Sq. West, Garth shows up in muddy coveralls driving a very muddy GMC dually truck. He had been working on a bull dozer he owned and forgot about the time. The day he signed my FG-180 he was dressed in his stage attire and had Sandi and Bob Doyle with him. The next time he was in my office I had this small toy guitar that Jerry Bradley had put into a dirty Santa game during our Christmas party at the Opryland Hotel. I wound up with the guitar and was trying to adjust the strings when Garth walks in and starts fooling with it....Alan Mayor was in the building for an event with his camera and shot a picture after Garth signed ..."God Bless...Garth Brooks"....Doug Supernaw who was a recording artist then and happen to walk off the elevator at the time jumped into our picture.. I have many other stories about Garth, Bob and ASCAP which will remain only a memory and may show up later in another book....

Chapter 17
Johnny Cash

As I sit this morning listening to the Folsom Prison Blues album by Johnny Cash, I reflect back to the day Johnny signed my guitar and how our lives related to each other with my adopted daughter Tanner Marie Long.

Figure 17 - Johnny Cash and Tom

Back on November 28th 1984 a little girl was born in the Baptist Hospital in Nashville, the same hospital where Johnny died. The mother was the daughter of Johnny Cash's sister. Prior to giving birth she decided to give up the baby for adoption. She used a doctor that Belinda knew and also knew one of the employees that worked there who was on the top of a list to get the next child available for adoption. Two weeks prior to Tanner's birth, Belinda's friend found out that she was with child and ask Belinda if she would like to take her spot on the list. Belinda was unable to have children and was very excited to say the least. Needless to say, I wasn't too sure about this decision since I already had two children from another marriage. On a trip to Mobile, Alabama to see Belinda's parents for Thanksgiving, I gave my ok and two weeks later we had Tanner Marie Long in our house on Woodlawn Drive in Nashville. We got her so suddenly that the only name we could think of was Belinda's maiden name, Tanner. Our Sunday school class at Park Ave. Baptist Church was great coming to our aid giving us a baby bed and blankets. Also, ASCAP gave us a great shower and Francis Preston, the head of BMI at he time, had her dad hand make a small rocking chair with Tanner's name and birth date painted on the chair along with bears and balloons. I was shocked the day Francis personally delivered the rocker to ASCAP, getting me out of a staff meeting on a Monday morning to present the gift. I think Connie Bradley, my boss, was more surprised that me that her competitor would do such a thing for an ASCAP rep.... After 28 years Tanner has matured with each year of her life and has given us a great looking grandson, Mason. They are living down in Georgia now near us in the Kennesaw area and doing well. The only sad part of this story is the fact that Tanner's biological mother has never agreed to meet her only daughter. Tanner wanted so much to meet her biological grandmother as well, but it never happened before she died.

Back in 1988 Rosanne Cash had a #1 song called "Tennessee Flattop Box". She claimed she didn't know her dad, Johnny, wrote the song until she recorded it. ASCAP had a #1 party for Johnny, who was an ASCAP writer, and this is where I got to spend some time with him and Rosanne. After the celebration, Johnny gladly agreed to sign my guitar and allow a picture to be made of that moment.

Chapter 18
Randy Travis

Randy is an interesting Carolina boy who made good. A rebel youth that was surely headed for prison had it not been for a married lady much older named Lib Hatcher. Randy grew up in Hendersonville, North Carolina and his real name was Randy Traywick. Randy performed one night in a club that Lib managed and she was stuck by his vocal talent and decided to help him out of his trouble with the law...

Figure 18 - Randy Travis and Tom

To keep Randy out of prison she convinced the judge to let her take control of his life, moved him into her home with her husband Frank, which later caused a divorce. Lib always had a plan after she met Randy to move to Nashville and shop for a record deal. Randy got a job washing dishes at the Nashville Palace near Opryland and Lib worked at the club as well. When the house band took a break each night Lib would get Randy out of the kitchen and sing a couple songs to keep the crowd entertained. During this process he would hang out on the sofa at ASCAP meeting writers and music row executives and later signed a publishing deal with Charlie Monk, the so called Mayor of Music Row. Later on Charlie would sell all of Randy's early songs which were just guitar vocals to Lib Hatcher for a several thousand dollars. Word got around that Randy had this very unique low country voice and Martha Sharpe from Warner Bros. Records went to see him at the Nashville Palace and signed him to an album deal. His first record , "Storms Of Life", was a smash and his music brought the country market back to the forefront thanks to great songs he recorded by Paul Overstreet and Don Schlitz such as "On The Other Hand".

Bob Doyle signed Randy to ASCAP before Garth came down the pike and we had numerous # 1 party gatherings for him. On one such celebration, Randy signed my guitar and I got a great photo that day. I would venture to say that without Lib Hatcher, Randy Travis would never have made it in country music. He would probably still be in prison somewhere in North Carolina. Lib had a great business head and married Randy after he became successful. Many people seemed to think that Randy was gay and only married Lib to cover up that fact.

This past year Randy and Lib divorced which made the news everywhere. Many jokes have been made around music row for years about their situation but no one has ever discounted the fact that Randy was the one singer that stood Country music back upon its feet in the late 1980's..Randy is still out there today somewhat wandering in the music wilderness acting in bit parts for movies and T.V. and trying his best to fit into a younger and different music generation...

Chapter 19
Clint Black

Clint Black was the one artist/writer on RCA Records that everyone thought looked like Roy Rogers. He first hit the scene in 1989 out of Houston, Texas after he started working with Bill Hamm who managed ZZ Top. Bill was able to land Clint a deal on RCA and his first album "Killin' Time" went platinum and produced 5 number one singles. When he released his 2nd album "Put Yourself In My Shoes", he rode his tour bus up and down music row promoting his new release. One of the stops was at ASCAP. At the time ASCAP was in a temporary building which was the old Merritt Music Space which later became the Polygram Records building and today is used by SESAC. Clint and some of the RCA people came into our office handing out a few samples of the new release and this gave me the opportunity to have Clint play and sign my guitar. I got two great pictures of him doing this and afterwards he scratched his famous name into the wood of my FG-180 red label Yamaha. A year or so later during a number one album party for Clint at the Stockyards restaurant parking

Figure 19 - Clint Black and Tom

lot, I was present and watched my friend and Clint's producer James Stroud give him a Porche 911 as a gift for taking his song "Where Are You Now" and "Loving Blind" to the top of the charts and selling one million records..

Chapter 20
Johnny Lee

Johnny Lee was born with the name John Lee Ham in July of 1946 in Alta Loma, Texas. He was raised on a dairy farm and had a band during high school called the Roadrunners. He served a tour in the navy and later started singing cover tunes in night clubs around Texas. He worked 10 years at Gilley's Club and hit a home run in 1980 with "Looking For Love In All The Wrong Places" which was a big part of the movie Urban Cowboy. He had a few more hits such as "One In A Million", "Bet Your Heart On Me", and "The Yellow Rose". He was on top of the world after the movie and rode that hit wave for several years , then settled down in Branson, Missouri. It was during the number one party of "Looking For Love" at the old ASCAP building that I got to meet Johnny and he was more than happy to sign my guitar. "Looking For Love" was an interesting story. Two school teacher down in Mississippi were writing songs and happened to send one up to Combine Music in Nashville. Bob Morrison a staff writer there received the song and felt it

Figure 20 - Johnny Lee and Tom

had potential and added his craftsmanship to the lyric and later pitched it to Johnny for the soundtrack of Urban Cowboy. Timing is everything in the music business as long as you're in the right place when the need arises....

Chapter 21
Reba McEntire

Better known today as just Reba. Her name was so universal that I named a collie pup Reba because when she held her ears up, she reminded me so much of the singer with all that shiny red glow hair. Reba had always been an ASCAP member ever since she started singing. As an ASCAP membership rep. it was my job to hang out in the clubs and shows to give support to artist and writer members and to sign up and coming Want-A-Be's.

Figure 21 - Reba McEntire and Tom

Reba's career has been long, big and seems to keep on growing because she's always up for a challenge. I think she has been one the the best Mc's of the CMA awards show and paired with Vince Gill made magic.

One morning at the old Pancake Pantry restaurant in Hillsboro Village I noticed Reba and her 1st husband Charlie Battles sitting over in a corner having pancakes. As I was checking out paying my bill I told David the owner to put their tab on my bill since ASCAP was paying. I also told David not to say anything other than her PRO bought her breakfast. I didn't think anything else about it until a couple weeks later I get a note in the mail addressed to me from some town in West Virginia. I opened the envelope and there was this big round belt buckle note card that had REBA in big letters on the front. The note said thanks for breakfast and it's on me the next time. I think she was sitting in a motel signing pictures and sending out thank you notes to everyone who had helped her in some way during the last several weeks. Little things like that is what's kept her on top all these years.

At another number one party for a song that Reba co-wrote she signed my guitar and I was able to get a couple of pictures.

When I was inducted into the Atlanta Country Music Hall of Fame back in 2000, the Columbia Tennessee Herald newspaper used that photo in an article about me when I lived in Santa Fe, Tn. on a small farm.

A good friend of mine, Ken Biddy, married Shelia Shipley who was the head of promotions at MCA Records which was Reba's label at the time. Reba gave Shelia a wedding shower at her horse farm near Mount Juliet,Tn. one evening and Belinda was invited. She arrived early at Reba's house and Reba gave my lovely wife the grand tour of her beautiful home and she got to see her son Shelby at age 5 trying to play the piano. So there you have it....Reba not only touched my life during our 30 years in Nashville, she also touched my wife's life as well....

Chapter 22
Bob McDill

The seasoned writer that most looked up to when I first hit music row back in 1981. He was the Mark Twain of country music and wrote a great deal of his hits alone which was a great asset when you got your royalty check out of the mail box.

Figure 22 - Bob McDill and Tom

When I first met Bob he was a staff

writer at Welk Music on the row. Bob did co-write some with his close friends but was hard pressed to write with an up and coming new artist. Bob has a literature degree from Lamar University in Texas and played in a skiffle band, called the Newcomers. His first cut was in 1967 by Perry Como and he thought he would have a career in pop music. His friend, Dickie Lee, persuaded him to move to Nashville however, and other friends like Allen Reynolds and cowboy Jack Clements gave him a launching pad to get his country songs recorded. Hits started happening like "Catfish John" by Johnny Russell, "Amanda" by Waylon Jennings and Don Williams, "Gone Country" by Alan Jackson, and many number 1's by Don Williams like "Good Ole' Boys Like Me".

Bob was one of BMI's biggest earning writers and one year in the early 90's he decided to switch to ASCAP and move his entire catalog of songs. Bob was a very smart person and figured out that in the long run his catalog would be worth more if being a part of the ASCAP family. When this move was completed ASCAP did a party and I got Bob to sign my FG-180 along with a great shot of the opportunity. Bob retired from writing songs in 2000 and started writing articles for magazines. Bob is a member of the Nashville Songwriters Hall of fame and ASCAP presented him with the Voice Award at their awards dinner in October 2012 celebrating 50 years of being in Nashville..

Chapter 23
Brad Paisley

Back in 1993 prior to me leaving ASCAP to accept a position with Anne Murray's company Balmur Entertainment, ASCAP had an intern from Belmont college, a young West Virginia Lad, Brad Paisley. He was there to learn the performing rights aspects of the music industry. He would sit in on meetings with other writers when thy came to the office and sit in on staff meetings. He helped any of the membership reps with busy work and often attended the album release parties and # 1 parties. All this was to earn school credits at Belmont in the commercial music program.

Figure 23 - Brad Paisley and Tom

One day Brad was in my office and we were talking and I ask him if he played an instrument, sang or wrote songs. He said yes, all of the above.. Well, my old FG-180 was on the guitar stand next to my desk and I ask him to play me something. He said no, that's not what I'm here for which made me reply back....pick up the guitar and play me a song.. In Brad's book "Diary Of A Player" on page 150 he says I told him to "play me a damn song or your fired". I don't recall saying it just like that, however, he finally picked up my guitar and played one of his original songs and knocked me over. I had John Briggs, another ASCAP rep, come into my office to listen and then I had the whole staff come in to listen. This was the seed planted that day which led to Chris DuBois who was a new rep. at ASCAP that lead to his dad Tim DuBois President of Arista Records which years later led to a record deal...Chris started writing songs with Brad which ultimately led to Chris leaving ASCAP to form a publishing company with Brad and Frank Rogers (Sea Gayle Music). Frank who was a student friend of Brad's became Brad's producer and Chris was the main publishing head. In 2010 and 2011 Sea Gayle was named the ASCAP Publisher Of The Year. What was strange about is that they are an independent publishing house and Chris's dad ,Tim, was the head of the ASCAP office for those two years...I think they won that honor fair and square because Brad had so many singles out and they were able to land many other outside cuts as well. The seed I planted that day back when Brad was just a Belmont student became a huge money tree and has made many people other than myself financially wealthy..

At the end of 1993, I was being interviewed for a position with Anne Murray's company, Balmur Entertainment, as V.P. of publishing. This came about thru my attorney friend, Steven Gladstone, who called me up one day and asked if I would be interested in interviewing for the job. I agreed and flew to Toronto, Canada to meet Leonard Rambo, Anne's manager. More about this in the next chapter...

About this time I knew I was probably leaving ASCAP, and I gave Brad Paisley one more job before I would leave. I ask him to transcribe all the signatures that were scratched into the grain of my guitar and put them in alphabetical order. This took about three days and he finally finished with the help of a magnifying glass. Brad typed these into a computer and the total was 203 signatures. He did a great job and the list is included in this book. Many of the ones that signed my guitar have passed away and many I was unable to get a picture with at the time of the signing. You'll notice the list says 204 now since Brad Signed.

After Brad had done all this work for me he asked if I would like to see his scrap book. I said sure, and the next day he brings in this huge book with all these pictures of him opening for different acts in West Virginia and one where he was inducted into the Wheeling West Virginia Music Hall Of Fame. I was very impressed and knew there was something very special about his kid. He gave me a West Virginia College T-Shirt and I told him that one day he would be a big star and I would then let him sign my guitar. Years later I attended his first #1 party and Brad signed my guitar and the picture is included in this book. After I moved back to Georgia to take care of my mother, Brad signed a document for me attesting to the fact that he transcribed all the names from my guitar and he also signed my copy of his book....Diary Of A Player.......I was very proud that our lives touched back in the early part of the 1990's and so glad that Brad has become not only a great artist, player, and song

writer, but a very faith oriented family
man who has not let outside forces
control his focus and life...

Chapter 24

Anne Murray

I have worked for four Legends in the music Industry. Bill Lowery, Buddy Killen, Hal David, and Anne Murray. I have mentioned the first three already and I thought Anne would be the last boss I would ever have in this great business. Unfortunately, it only lasted six years and I was very disappointed. Anne was great to me as was her manager Leonard Rambo. As I stated earlier, Mr. Rambo, who is the same age as Anne and I, flew me to Toronto for a meeting or interview for the position at Balmur Entertainment.

Figure 24 - Anne Murray, Tom and guests

I checked into the Marriott there at the airport and a limo was to pick me up and drive me to the Balmur Music office. Belinda had packed me a suit to wear, and after I put it on, I just didn't feel right. I pulled it off, put my jeans on with my cowboy boots and a sports jacket and caught the limo headed down Younge street to meet Mr. Rambo. Leonard had me to come into his office, I sat down and listened to him talk for about one hour about the company, how he met Anne, how he never had a written contract with her, only a hand shake deal and their plans for Nashville. I bet I didn't say 20 words the whole hour. I immediately liked Leonard and his style. He stood up from his desk and ask me the question--- How would you like to work for Anne Murray? I said it would be an honor and then he said----Welcome aboard---All I could say was ----WOW—That was easy, however the hard part was lying months down the road.

I gave Connie Bradley, the head of the Nashville ASCAP office, my letter of resignation and started to work for Balmur Entertainment the beginning of

1994. The letters in the word BALMUR came from three sources....The B was from Bill, Anne husband, A from Anne, and L from Leonard and of course the MUR from Murray. I had been with ASCAP for 10 years and I was scared to death taking on a new venture with such a super star. Going into this new gig as Vice President of Publishing gave me an instant $10,000 a year salary increase from $65,000 to $75,000 and would reach $100,000 during my final year. I was promised stock options, which never happened and after the first 2 years of building the company, Leonard Rambo died of cancer. Anne now had a new manager, Bruce Allen, a new President of the company, Tony Bayliss, who I did not see eye to eye with me on several issues and in 2000 my contract came up for renewal and Tony decided not to pick up my option. The main reason for this was the fact that I would not go along with him cooking the income numbers in order to give the company a higher value in order to sell to Chorus Music in Canada. When I told him I could not forecast a higher income stream that just wasn't in the pipeline, he wasn't very happy and therefore I lost my job. No matter if I had stayed ,the hand writing was on the wall that Balmur was going to sell out and my future there would be short lived.

During those six years with Anne Murray, we had 10 #1 songs in various charts and over 300 cuts by different artists in the U.S. and Canada. The great thing about those six years is that I learned first hand a lot about music publishing and got to visit France for the International music conference and got to travel to many parts of Canada. I also played golf with Anne in a huge Skins game golf tournament at Prince Edward Island with John Daly, Mark O'Meara, Fred Couples and Mike Weir. What an awesome time and experience that was just to hang with those guys and have dinner together. I guess the most rewarding time however, was getting to take my dad to Calgary to the Canadian Country Music Awards. He had such a great time seeing the Rockies, Lake Louise, and all the huge Elk. He also got to eat pizza with Terri Clark in the Chicago airport while waiting to change planes. He thought that was really cool.

Anne would come to Nashville a few times a year to check on things and see how her house and company was doing at 1105 17th Ave. She had a condo in Green Hills where she would stay while in town doing business and I was able on several occasions to have her included in pictures when I would sign various writers such as Kim Tribble, and Alaska's Hobo Jim. During one of her visits to renew my contract for my final 3 years Anne signed my guitar and I was able to get a couple of personal camera shots of the honor.. Anne was a great boss and has remained a friend. I usually call her at Christmas and on her birthday which is June 20th. She, like Leonard Rambo and I, were born the same year, 1945.

One last story about Anne which I think is necessary for this book...After going to work for her in January 1994, I was invited to her Christmas party in December of that year at the Thornhill Country Club in Toronto. It was freezing that day and I was down with a cold, but flew up anyway and found myself to be the only American at the party. She had everyone that had anything to do with her business or career there that night. I guess there were about 50 people from hair dressers, booking agents, band members, engineers and attorneys. I sat with Anne at her table and they had two door prizes to be given away. One was drawn from a hat and the prize was two round tickets to London ,England. The other prize was a Thousand Dollar Bill. Who ever had a certain number under their place mat won that prize. I won both prizes and everyone in the room could have killed me. Rigged, rigged, some said and I really felt uncomfortable, so I gave the London tickets back and let them do another drawing. I kept the Canadian Thousand Dollar Bill which turned out to be only about $760.00 U.S. A few weeks after the party Anne sent me a picture of all of us at the table with me holding up the large thousand dollar bill and she wrote a note on the picture.....you lucky S.O.B. When Anne retired she wrote a book called "All Of Me" and mentioned me under the publishing section. What a classic voice, a classy lady and a pretty good golfer.

Chapter 25
Pat Boone

After my tenure with Anne Murray, Donna HIlley, who was the President of SonyATV Music, formerly Tree Publishing, called me one day and ask if I would consider coming back to work there to oversee the Bill Lowery catalog which they had just purchased for many millions of dollars. I heard it was between 20 & 40 Million... I was thrilled and accepted the offer and was glad to be back at my old stomping grounds. I knew most all the songs very well since my career started with the Lowery Group . While reviewing the catalog I discovered some Don Carroll Gospel songs that I had never heard before. His voice reminded me of Pat Boone and the thought struck me to maybe do a Gospel

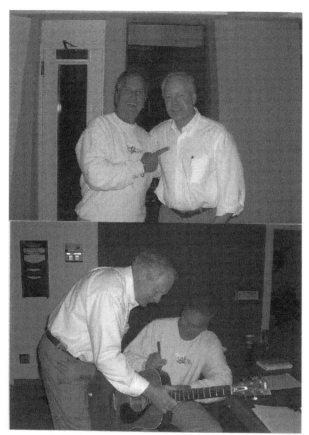
Figure 25 - Pat Boone and Tom

Record on Pat of some of Don's songs and
maybe some other SonyATV copyrights. I
approached Donna about the idea and she
agreed. I got in touch with Mr. White
Shoes and he agreed as well, so I started a
song search and got Pat McMakin, the
studio manager at Sony, to help me
produce the project. We flew Pat Boone
in for a week, gave him a great advance,

made some pictures, got the Jordanaires to sing back up and cut 15 sides. Pat had done many Gospel albums for his own label and Curb Records. Mike Curb was a big fan and friend of Pat, so he picked up our album, gave us a $15,000 advance and I was thrilled until........I had put so much time and effort into making this album happen, spend $700 shooting pictures of Pat and gave all the credits and great photos to Curb and was sure the album would look awesome.

When the album came out, it had a picture of an old church on the front, and no credits listed at all...Not my name, not Pat McMakin's name, not the Jordanaires, and only the song titles. I was pretty ticked to say the least....The last time I checked, the album had only sold less than 100 copies. Anyway, I had a great time with another Legend who went to lunch with me everyday and agreed to sign my FG-180. He was very professional, kind, generous but had lost much of his singing chops, however, thanks to Pro Tools he was spot on after many hours of work....

Chapter 26
The Kentucky Headhunters

My book would not be complete if I didn't do a chapter on the one band that I have spend more time with than any other artist or writer. Formerly called Ichy Brother in their younger days, inspired from a cartoon character. I first met Richard Young, Fred Young, and Anthony Kenny back in 1976 when I worked at Perfection Sound Studios. They were passing thru Georgia doing some shows and invited Larry Latimer and I up to Kentucky to see a show of theirs at a County Fair. When we arrived they were playing in a tent next to a dirt track where cars were flying around in a circle with no mufflers. Fred the drummer arrived with no shirt sitting in the back seat of an old 1948 4 door chevy with big Dave, their roadie, driving. Fred gets out of the car with his two drum sticks and marches into the tent where the other band members are waiting...They put on a great show and actually were louder than the stock cars.

Larry and I felt we could help these young rock and rollers, so we moved them to Smyrna, Georgia. They were all living in a two bedroom apartment and we started booking them in high schools, colleges, and trying our best to get enough publicity to entice a record label to sign them...They signed a production agreement with Star Quest Attractions and after one year decided to move back to Kentucky...Richard and Fred were brothers who lived on a 1200 acres farm in Edmonton ,Ky, and Anthony lived in Glasglow. At the time they had a red headed bass player by the name of Tim Speck... He didn't last very long and after several years of trying different names they finally decided on the Kentucky Headhunters. I signed them to ASCAP and one night I drove Harold Shedd, Buddy Cannon, Jim Zumwalt and Craig Hayes up to Bowling Green, Ky. in my 1986 Astro Van to hear them play at a small club called Picausso's. We were about 1 hour late and the place was packed with their local fans...On the way back to Nashville, Harold fired up a huge joint and started passing it around saying Tom...Should I sign these boys?...I had my window rolled

Figure 26 - Kentucky Head Hunters & Tom

down so I could breathe, and kept
answering,,,,if you don't you're gonna
miss out on something big...We pulled
over at a truck stop for coffee and I think
with everyone agreeing they were tight,
very unique and different enough look
wise that the new generation of country
fans would probably buy their records I
think their first single "Walk Softly On
This Heart Of Mine" written by Bill
Monroe was so unique sounding that it
turned heads all the way to the Grammy
and CMA awards....To date I think they
have sold around 8 million albums and
my wife and I had the joy of being in their
first video of "Walk Softly".....Man was it

hot that day in the top of an old dairy barn on their dad's farm.

Rewind back to SonyATV.. After my Pat Boone record was done I had the bright idea to do an album with the Kentucky Headhunters of all Sony standards. This would give Sony a chance to have different versions of some great old songs and maybe a shot at some movies or commercials. Donna Hilley agreed and I picked out about 40 songs for the boys to hear and we started recording in Glasglow, Ky. at one of their friends studios....The album was called "Big Boss Man" and that was their first single. We shot a video of the song at a coal mine in Kentucky and the album contains 15 of those 40 songs that I chose for them to review.

The Kentucky Headhunters put out another album called "Flying Under The Radar" which contained a few of those songs we recorded and I was the only person to ever co-produce a record with the Kentucky Headhunters. For some reason, I never got any of the Headhunters to sign my guitar. They had signed so many other things for me, I guess I just overlooked those many opportunities even after they had played my guitar so many times...

SAMMY JOHNS
CHAPTER 27

Just as I was finishing this book I got an email from John Conlee's assistant, Diane Cash, in Nashville telling me she just heard that Sammy Johns had passed away. My heart immediately felt sad because he had been on my mind for several days to call and before I got around to it, he was gone.

(John Conlee, Sammy Johns, Tom Long)

Sammy and I met back in the mid 70's right after his song "Chevy Van" was a huge pop hit. Larry Latimer introduced me to him and we became friends. After I went to work for Bill Lowery I was able to get Sammy signed there as a writer which started our long relationship. Sammy wrote a song called "Common Man" and I introduced him to James Stroud who was managing the Web IV studios in Atlanta where Paul Davis was a writer and artist for Bang Records. Ed Seay was the engineer and we were able to cut some sides on Sammy which later came out as singles on Southern Tracks Records owned by Bill Lowery. The most important song back then to me was "Common Man" that Stroud and I produced at Studio One owned by Buddy Buie and Mr. Lowery and the engineer was Rodney Mills of 38 Special Fame. Larry Latimer had given Sammy a line for the song without any credit which was "I'd rather chug-a-lug a mug of Budwiser Beer than sip a crystal glass of wine" which to me was the best line in the whole song. While we were cutting the demo, I told Sammy I felt the song needed a bridge and gave him the following lines while we were recording, (I'm happy just being free, and I'm happy just being me, and I hope that you will see). Sammy said cool, and it went to tape. I didn't think anything about taking any writer credit at the time but years later I wished I had given that more thought since it became a three millions performance song at BMI.

"Common Man" came out as a single, with Sammy singing, on Elektra Records and died at #50 on the Billboard charts produced by me and James Stroud. I was working at Tree Publishing at that point in 1981 and was sitting in my office feeling down listening to the single once again. While listening, Bud Logan, John Conlee's record producer, walked by my office and heard the song playing. He stuck his head in my door and said, what song is that? I told him "Common Man" by Sammy Johns and it just stiffed at #50. Bud said, make me a copy, I think John Conlee will dig this and he's cutting his new album down in the Tree Studio. John loved it, recorded it, and it went straight to number one in the charts and became one of his most requested songs next to Rose Colored Glasses.

Along about this time Sammy wanted me to be his manager and I was doing all I could to help him. I hooked him up one day with Michael Garvin, a tree writer, and they wrote "Desperato Love:" which Conway Twitty took to number one and later on Waylon Jennings cut Sammy's song "America" which was a big hit. Sammy was always calling me or writing me letters wanting me to help him in some way and I was able to get him on the Nashville Now Show with Ralph Emory and in June of 2010 I got Sammy on the Grand Ole Opry to sing "Common Man" with John Conlee. This was one of the highlights of Sammy's career next to being on American Bandstand with Dick Clark when Chevy Van was riding high in the Pop charts.

Sammy not only left his signature on my guitar but left this life way too early. He made his mark in the music world and his songs will live on, as long as there is a radio, an internet or a musician who fills his tip jar with request money.

CHAPTER 28
THREE SHORT STORIES CLOSE TO MY HEART

Chet Atkins and I played golf together a couple of times in the Jerry Chesnut "Closed Open" tournament held at the old Nashboro Village complex.

Chet Atkins
June 20, 1924 – June 30, 2001

He always had a female with him that was a guitar student, so he said, which gave our foursome a little more glamour. On one hole I had an eagle to put us a few strokes under par and Chet said "Tom, you're my hero". I often thought, man I wished I had that on tape. After the tournament, I asked Chet to sign my guitar and he refused saying he hated to damage a perfectly good guitar. I insisted, so he did put his initials on it...just C.A.

Lee Greenwood had his first #1 song because I stayed in the bathroom too long. I told this to Lee one day and he thought I was crazy, but it's true. Jerry Crutchfield, Lee's producer, called me one day and requested a song in the Tree catalog. Back then all the songs were on reel to reel, so I proceeded to make a cassette copy of the song and while it was recording I went to the bathroom. Someone detained me for a few minutes while washing my hands and when I got back to my office the next song on the reel behind the one Crutchfield wanted was also being recorded onto the cassette. I left the song on, pull a lyric sheet, and took both songs down to Mr. Crutchfield's office. Lee recorded the second song, "Somebody's Gonna Love You" written by

Don Cook and Rafe VanHoy, and it was
Lee Greenwood's first number one single.
After this, Rafe and Don both signed my
guitar and took my wife and I to dinner.

I have always been a cowboy at heart,
owning horses and visiting the west as
often as possible.

(Johnny Cash, Kathy Mattea, Gene & Tom)

My first guitar was a Gene Autry model
from Sears and Roebuck with Gene and
his horse Champion on the front. One
year Gene was the guest speaker at the

ASCAP awards in Nashville and I had the honor to escort him around prior to the event so various artists could get their pictures made with him. We had a great discussion concerning that early guitar and I told him about my FG-180 and he said he would have loved to sign it, but unfortunately it was back at my office that night. We talked about Pasty Montana who wrote and sang " I Want To Be A Cowboy's Sweetheart" and he told me that her first movie was with him in Colorado Sunset. Pasty stopped by ASCAP one day a few years prior to that night checking on her royalties and signed my guitar and surprised me by playing and singing "I Want To Be A Cowboy's Sweetheart'". After she left the building I was in awe that she had sang that song while playing my guitar...

Chapter 29
In Closing

Hand to hand my guitar has helped me fulfill many of my dreams and gave me much comfort over the years whether just giving me peace of mind when I played it or watching someone famous make their mark in her maple wood grain. Yes, I must say that this old FG-180 red label Yamaha can truly talk and tell many soul soothing stories. Those artists and writers that signed it but not mentioned in my book will have to remain silent in the wood grain to be told at a later time and day. However, there is one kid who never signed it that worked for me at Balmur Entertainment that I had to let go or fire after only working for four months. He was my tape copy person who came to work everyday dressed like he was ready to go on stage and sing. He was from Ada, Oklahoma and moved to Nashville right out of high school to chase his singing dream. He had a huge laugh, love to hunt and had very long hair under his cowboy hat and he stood 6 foot 5 inches tall. He turned out to be a terrible tape copy person but I knew there was a special aura about him that could turn into something special and big. With this in the back of my mind I gave him a song that I had a personal income interest in and told him he should record it if he ever got a record deal. I let him go from Balmur, to chase that dream and he did record the song "Ole Red" which I gave him and he is currently on top of the world in country music and one of the judges on the T.V. show "The Voice". Blake Shelton, knew what he wanted most of his life, skipped college and went for the brass ring. He still has a firm hold that will most likely last for many years to come.

As I stated earlier, a complete list of all signatures on my guitar are included in the back of this book and with Alan Mayor's permission all the pictures taken of artists and writers signing my guitar. There are many famous names here that were not mentioned in this book, however one can see their names on the list as well as the many that have passed on but whose memory will live on thru their music.

Thanks for reading "This Guitar Can Talk" and hopefully you have learned some untold music details that have never been reported before...Many people often say, If only these wall could talk....Well the walls of this old FG-180 Yahama have spoken and hopefully a few ears are listening....God Bless ....

Tom Long or as my mother calls me....Tommy Lee Long

**TOM LONG'S AUTOHGRAPHED
GUITAR SIGNATURES**

1. DENNIS ADKINS......WROTE "ACE IN THE HOLE' FOR GEORGE STRAIT
2. DEBORAH ALLEN......FORMER RCA ARTIST
3. BOBBY BARE....COUNTRY LEGEND
4. JOE BARNHILL.....FORMER CAPITOL ARTIST
5. TED BARTON.....SONG PLUGGER FOR MCA
6. CRAIG BICKHARDT....WELL KNOWN MUSIC ROW WRITER
7. CLINT BLACK.....TEXAS SUPERSTAR
8. BOBBY BORCHERS.....MUSIC ROW WRITER
9. JESSICA BOUCHER

10. LARRY BOWIE....ATLANTA WRITER
ARTIST
11. PAT BOONE....MUSIC ICON
12. ALICIA BRIDGES...ARTIST ON "I LOVE
THE NIGHTLIFE"
13. GARTH BROOKS...BEST SELLING
COUNTRY ARTIST OF ALL TIME
14. LANE BRODY...FORMER CAPITOL ARTIST
15. RAZZY BALIEY...GREAT COUNTRY
ARTIST WHO WROTE "9,999,999 TEARS
16. LARRY BUTLER....1ST PRODUCER TO WIN
GRAMMY FROM NASHVILLE
17. PAMELA A. BROWN..MUSIC ROW
WRITER
18. T. GRAHAM BROWN...FORMER CAPITOL
ARTIST...
19. JAMES BURTON...GUITAR PLAYER FOR
ELVIS AND RICKY NELSON
20. BYRD (BARRY BURTON)...PRODUCER OF
THE AMAZING RHYTHM ACES
21. LANA CANTRELL
22. BRUCE CARROLL...AWARDING WINNING
GOSPEL ARTIST...
23. JOHNNY CARLISLE...ATLANTA BASED
GUITAR PLAYER
24. COTTON CARRIER...HOST OF WSB
BARNDANCE IN ATLANTA/ AND FIRST
TO BOOK ELVIS IN ATLANTA AND
WORKED FOR THE LOWERY GROUP
25. JOHNNY CASH.....LEGEND
26. HOWARD CHADWICK
27. BRUCE CHANNEL...WRITER AND ARTIST
ON HIT "HEY BABY"
28. BETH NIELSEN CHAPMAN...WARNER
BROS. ARTIST.....

29. GARY CHAPMAN..HOST OF NASHVILLE NOW AND GOSPEL ARTIST
30. JERRY CHESNUT...HALL OF FAME WRITER
31. TERY CHOATE...NASHVILLE PRODUCER
32. JOHNNY CHRISTOPHER...WRITER OF "YOU WERE ALWAYS ON MY MIND"
33. J.R. COBB...MEMBER OF THE ATLANTA RHYTHM SECTION
34. HANK COCHRAN...HALL OF FAME WRITER
35. WILLIS COLEMAN
36. JOHN CONLEE..MCA ARTIST WHO MADE ROSE COLORED GLASSES FAMOUS
37. STEVE CROPPER...WRITER OF "MIDNIGHT HOUR"
38. JEFF CROSSAN..WRITER OF "TIME OFF FOR BAD BEHAVIOR"
39. SONNY CURTIS....MEMBER OF THE CRICKETS
40. DEAN DAUGHTRY...MEMBER OF THE ATLANTA RHYTHM SECTION
41. GAIL DAVIES ....FORMER CAPITOL ARTIST
42. DELORES DEAL
43. MIKE DEKLE..WRITER OF SCARLETT FEVER"
44. JOE DIFFIE..EPIC ARTIST
45. DEAN DILLION...SONGWRITER WHO WROTE MANY GEORGE STRAIT HITS
46. LOLA JEAN DILLON...WRITER FOR MANY LORETTA LYNN HITS
47. STEVE DORFF...L.A. WRITER
48. JIM DOWELL
49. BARRY ETRES..WROTE "RUBAN JAMES"

50. DON EVERLY...ONE OF THE FAMOUS EVERLY BROTHERS
51. SAMMY FAIN...CLASSIC TEN PAN ALLEY WRITER
52. DICK FELLER..WROTE "EAST BOUND AND DOWN"
53. JOHNNY FEW
54. GEORGE FOX....CANADIAN COUNTRY ARTIST
55. MICHAEL GARVIN...HIT MUSIC ROW WRITER
56. DON GOODMAN....WROTE "RING ON HER FINGER TIME ON HER HANDS"
57. BOB GAUDIO...WROTE THE FOUR SEASONS HITS
58. FLASH GORDON
59. MICHELLE GREENE...HOLLYWOOD ACTRESS SINGER
60. LEE GREEWOOD...WRITER OF "GOD BLESS THE U.S.A.
61. JIMMY GRIFFIN   MEMBER OF THE GROUP BREAD
62. RICHARD GROSSMAN...
63. EDGEL GROVES... SINGER OF 'FOOTPRINTS IN THE SAND"
64. HILLARY KANTER,,,FORMER RCA ARTIST.....
65. LARRY HALL
66. ISSAC HAYES...STAXS RECORDS ICON AND MOVIE STAR
67. CHIP HARDY
68. SHAWNA HARRINGTON
69. EMMYLOU HARRIS...COUNTRY SUPERSTAR
70. J.D. HART

71. ROY HEAD...COUNTRY ARTIST
72. AUDI HENRY
73. DON HENRY...CO-WRITER ON
   "WHERE'VE YOU BEEN"
74. BYRON HILL...MUSIC ROW FAMOUS
   WRITER
75. KENNY HINSON...GOSPEL ARTIST
76. BERTIE HIGGINS..ARTIST AND WRITER
   OF "KEY LARGO"
77. TOMMY HOLCOMB...COMMERCIAL
   PRODUCER
78. JAN HOLLIER...TEXAS ARTIST....
79. HARLAN HOWARD..HALL OF FAME
   WRITER
80. CON HUNLEY...COUNTRY ARTIST
81. SUSAN HUTCHINGSON..CO-WRITER OF "I
   LOVE THE NIGHTLIFE"
82. MARK IRWIN...WRITER OF "HERE IN THE
   REAL WORLD"
83. ALAN JACKSON..COUNTRY SUPERSTAR
84. WAYLON JENNINGS...COUNTRY ICON
85. SAMMY JOHNS...POP ARTIST OF CHEVY
   VANN
86. DOUG JOHNSON...WRITER/LABEL HEAD
   AND PRODUCER
87. BUCKY JONES...MUSIC ROW WRITER
88. CARL JACKSON...MUSIC ROW
   WRITER/PRODUCER
89. BEN JONES..ACTOR IN DUKES OF
   HAZZARD
90. WYNONNA JUDD.....SINGER OF THE
   JUDDS
91. KIERAN KANE..WRITER AND ARTIST IN
   NASHVILLE

92. ANGELA KASSET...SESAC WRITER OF
THE YEAR
93. SAMMY KERSHAW...MERCURY ARTIST
94. BUDDY KILLEN...FORMER OWNER OF
TREE PUBLISHING
95. DAVE KING
96. DON KING...ARTIST/WRITER IN
NASHVILLE
97. RICHARD KLENDER
98. FRANK KNAPP....WRITER/ACTOR
99. FRED KNOBLOCH...MUSIC ROW WRITER
AND FORMER ARTIST
100.   TOM KNOX...ENGINEER
101.   MICHAELKOSSER,,,SONGWRITER/
BOOK AUTHOR
102.   RED LANE..HALL OF FAME
WRITER/GUITAR PLAYER
103.   ALAN LANEY...WRITER
104.   MIKE LANTRIP....ALABAMA
WRITER
105.   DICKEY LEE..HALL OF FAME
WRITER
106.   WOODY LEE...TEXAS BASED
ARTIST
107.   JOHNNY LEE...URBAN COWBOY
ARTIST....
108.   LATHAN HUDSON...WRITER OF
"NEW LOOKS FROM OLD LOVER"
109.   TONY MARTY
110.   WARNER MACK..COUNTRY
ARTIST
111.   GLEN MARTIN...MUSIC ROW
WRITER
112.   J.D. MARTIN...MUSIC ROW
WRITER

113.   WAYNE MASSEY...SOAP OPERA
STAR
114.   KATHY MATTEA..MERCURY
RECORDING ARTIST....
115.   TIM MCCABE...ATLANTA WRITER
PRODUCER
116.   REBA MCENTIRE....COUNTRY
SUPERSTAR
117.   BILLY EARL MCCLELLAN....BLUES
WRITER
118.   DELBERT MCCLINTON...POP
BLUES SUPERSTAR
119.   BOB MCDILL...HALL OF FAME
WRITER
120.   PAT MCMANUS...WRITER OF
"AMERICAN MADE"
121.   DANA MCVICKER....
122.   BOB MERRILL
123.   ROGER MILLER...COUNTRY
SUPERSTAR AND ICON
124.   ZELL MILLER...FORMER
GOVERNOR OF GEORGIA
125.   KATY MOFFATT...CMT HOST
126.   PASTY MONTANA..WRITER,
SINGER OF "COWGIRL'S SWEETHEART"
127.   BEN MOORE...BLUES SINGER
128.   RANDY MOORE
129.   DANNY
MORRISON...WRITER/MANAGER
130.   MICHAEL MARTIN
MURPHY...WESTERN ARTIST
131.   WILLIE NELSON....COUNTRY ICON
132.   HAL NEWMAN....
133.   ROBERT NIX...DRUMMER FOR
THE ATLANTA RHYTHM SECTION

134.   LEE OFFMAN
135.   TOM OCCHIPINI
136.   JAMIE O'HARA...MUSIC ROW HIT WRITER
137.   ORION...THE ONY MASKED COUNTRY MUSIC ARTIST....
138.   BUCK OWENS..COUNTRY SUPERSTAR
139.   MARK PADEN
140.   DOLLY PARDON...COUNTRY SUPERSTAR
141.   FLOYD PARTON...DOLLY'S BROTHER
142.   TOM PAXTON...WRITER ARTIST...
143.   ED PENNY...CO-WRITER OF "SOMEBODY'S KNOCKING"
144.   GINO PISTILLI....MUISC ROW WRITER
145.   ROYCE PORTER.....MUSIC ROW WRITER
146.   LEONARD POSTOSTIEO... LEONARD LOSERS RADIO SHOW
147.   SUE POWELL
148.   TONY PRESLEY
149.   CURLY PUTMAN...HALL OF FAME WRITER
150.   LEON RAINES...ALABAMA WRITER/ARTIST
151.   JERRY REED...COUNTRY SUPERSTAR
152.   ALAN RHODY...MUSIC ROW WRITER/ARTIST
153.   BILLY LEE RILEY...EARLY SUN RECORDS ARTIST....

154. JOHNNY RIVER...FAMOUS POP ARTIST....
155. KEN ROBBINS...FAMOUS MUSIC ROW WRITER
156. TOMMY ROE...POP SUPERSTAR, CO- WRITER OF DIZZY
157. PHIL SAMPOSN....
158. THETIS SEALEY
159. JOHN SCHNEIDER...BO DUKE OF THE DUKES OF HAZZARD
160. TROY SEALS...FAMOUS SONGWRITER
161. JEANNIE SEELEY...GRAND OLE OPRY STAR
162. JERRY LEE SHELFER...
163. T.G. SHEPPARD...COUNTRY SUPERSTAR
164. TOM SHAPIRO...BMI SONGWRITER OF THE YEAR
165. RICH SHULMAN
166. SHEL SILVERSTEIN...WRITER OF "ONE PIECE AT A TIME"
167. MARGO SMITH...COUNTRY ARTIST....
168. MIKE SNIDER...GRAND OLE OPRY STAR
169. JOE SOUTH. ATLANTA SONGWRITER..."ROSE GARDEN"
170. GARY STEWART...COUNTRY ARTIST
171. EVEN STEVENS...WRITER OF MANY EDDIE RABBIT'S HITS
172. RAY STEVENS...COUNTRY SUPERSTAR
173. NAT STUCKEY..COUNTRY ARTIST

174.   JOE SUN....COUNTRY ARTIST.....
175.   SONNY THROCKMORTON...HALL OF FAME WRITER
176.   DON TOLLE...MUSIC PUBLISHER
177.   MICHAEL TONE
178.   RANDY TRAVIS....COUNTRY SUPERSTAR
179.   TANYA TUCKER...COUNTRY SUPERSTAR
180.   JACK TURNER...ALTANTA BASED WRITER
181.   CONWAY TWITTY...COUNTRY/POP SUPERSTAR
182.   JON WALMSLEY...SON ON THE T.V. SHOW THE WALTONS
183.   RAFE VAN HOY....MUSIC ROW WRITER
184.   RANDY VAN WARNER...WRITER OF "JUST WHEN I NEEDED YOU
185.   MOST
186.   KEVIN WELCH...WRITER OF "TOO OLD TO DIE THIS YOUNG"
187.   FREDDY WELLER....ARTIST/WRITER, C0-WROTE "DIZZY"
188.   DOTTIE WEST....COUNTRY SUPERSTAR
189.   L.E. WHITE...MUISC ROW WRITER
190.   RAY WHITLEY...WRITER OF MANY TAMS HITS
191.   JAY REMINTON WILDE....MUSIC ROW WRITER
192.   DAVID WILLS...MUSIC ROW WRITER

193.   KIM WILLIAMS...WRITER OF
MANY OF GARTH BROOKS HITS
194.   GENE WATSON...COUNTRY
SUPERSTAR
195.   KEVIN WINN.
196.   MICHAEL WOODY
197.   BUD LEE....CO-WRITER OF
"FRIENDS IN LOW PLACES"
198.   JIM VARNEY...COMEDY ACTOR
199.   JON VEZNER...CO-WRITER OF
"WHERE'VE YOU BEEN"
200.   HANA YOVEL ..ISRAEL
SONGWRITER
201.   FARON YOUNG...COUNTRY MUSIC
SUPERSTAR
202.   ANNE MURRAY...CANADIAN
SUPERSTAR AND MY FORMER BOSS
203.   LARRY LATIMER...WRITER OF
THE JOHN DEERE COMMERICAL

204.   BRAD PAISLEY...MY INTERN AT
ASCAP WHO BECAME A COUNTRY
MUSIC SUPERSTAR

NOTE*** AS OF THIS WRITING 37 OF
THESE HAVE PASSED AWAY

Figure 27 - Tom at Mastersound Studios 1976

TOM LONG

TOM LONG HAS OVER THIRTY FIVE YEARS
EXPERIENCE AS A MUSIC BUSINESS
PROFESSIONAL. THIS GEORGIA NATIVE CO-
FOUNDED THE ATLANTA SONGWRITERS

ASSOCIATION IN THE LATE SEVENTIES WHILE
BEING EMPLOYED BY THE LOWERY MUISC
ORGANIZATION AND RECEIVED A
MANAGEMENT DEGREE FROM GEORGIA STATE
UNIVERSITY.

AFTER MOVING TO NASHVILLE IN 1981, TOM
SERVED AS THE PRESIDENT OF THE
NASHVILLE SONGWRITERS ASSOCIATION
WHLIE WORKING FOR TREE PUBLISHING
COMPANY WHERE HE WAS RESPONSIBLE FOR
SEVERAL NUMBER ONE RECORDS SUCH AS
"COMMON MAN" FOR JOHN CONLEE AND
"SOMEONE'S GONNA LOVE YOU" FOR LEE
GREENWOOD, "YOU'RE GONNA RUIN MY BAD
REPETITION" BY RONNIE MCDOWELL.

TOM SPEND A DECADE (1984 THRU 1994) AS
NASHVILLE DIRECTOR OF MEMBERSHIP FOR
ASCAP (AMERICAN SOCIETY OF COMPOSERS,
AUTHORS, AND PUBLISHERS) AND GRADUATED
FROM THE LEADSHIP MUSIC PROGRAM. ANNE
MURRAY HIRED TOM IN 1994 TO HEAD UP HER
PUBLISHING COMPANY, BALMUR
ENTERTAINMENT, AND DURING HIS SIX YEARS
THERE ENJOYED 10 NUMBER ONE SONGS IN
VARIOUS CHARTS.

IN 2001 SONYATV MUSIC ACQUIRED TOM TO
SERVE AS CATALOG MANAGER WHERE HE WAS
INSRUMENTAL IN THE PRODUCTION OF
SPECIAL PROJECTS FOR THE KENTUCKY
HEADHUNTERS, BRENDA LEE AND PAT BOONE
AMOUNG OTHERS.. CURRENTLY TOM IS

OWNER AND PRESIDENT OF HIS OWN
PUBLISHING COMPANY (THAT-A-FLY MUSIC)

PEOPLE I WISH TO THANK!

MY MUSICAL CAREER HAS BEEN TOUCHED B
SO MANY PEOPLE BUT THERE ARE SOME
SPECIAL ONES THAT ENCOURAGED AND
MADE MY JOURNEY POSSIBLE AND LITTLE
SMOOTHER ALONG THE WAY

Belinda Long, my awesome wife and her
family, Horace & Mildred Long, my sister
Genevieve and brother Monty, Bill Lowery, m
mentor in music publishing, Mary Tallent,
Cotton Carrier, Butch & Terri Lowery, Mike
Clark, Bob & Babs Richardson who gave me a
chance as an intern, Zell Miller who believed
me enough to put me on the original Ga. Mus
Hall of Fame committee, Buddy Killen who
hired me at Tree Publishing, Hal David, Conn
Bradley, Paul Adler and all the great folks at
ASCAP, Anne Murray, Leonard Rambo, Tinti
Moffat, Kim Tribble and the staff at Balmur
back in the 90's, Donna Hilley, Roger Sovine,
Troy Tomlinson, Jack Jackson, Adam Engleha
and all the great writers and staff at SonyAT
Music, The Kentucky Headhunter, David Fos
my former Pastor who passed away too earl

the Fly Nazarene Church who loved my family so much, Larry Latimer my soul brother in music, Mike Stewart, Danny Jones, Maggie Cavender who believed in me when I didn't, Tommy Jr., LaTease, and Tanner, my awesome children, Greg and Sheree Hanna, my Canadian family, Alaska's Hobo Jim, my wilderness brother, Rusty & Nona Jones, Steven Gladstone, Steven Weaver, John & Terri Colgin, Gary Duffy, Roger Wilson, Alan Mayor, Kim & Robbie Mathis, Peter Jenkins, Neda & Dick Brickner, Arnie & JoAnn Deckwa, Dallas & Susan Pearce and my Lord and Savior Jesus Christ...

Figure 28 - Horace, Mildred & Tom Long

Made in the USA
Columbia, SC
23 December 2023